Attracting Genuine Love

Sounds True, Inc., Boulder, CO 80306
© 2004 Gay and Kathlyn Hendricks

Published 2004
Printed in Korea

Gay and Kathlyn Hendricks
Attracting Genuine Love

ISBN 1-59179-171-5

Audio learning courses by Gay Hendricks available from Sounds True:
Ecstatic Sex
Fly without Fear
Seven Secrets of the Corporate Mystic

Drs. Kathlyn & Gay Hendricks

Attracting Genuine Love

SOUNDS TRUE

TABLE OF CONTENTS

Introduction

FOR MOST OF US, living without true love is not an option. What that true love looks like is ultimately up to us, but anyone can create a close, loving relationship, no matter what their past history or current situation is, if they understand certain key principles and learn a few skills. In fact, most people in the course of their day-to-day lives meet more than enough potential relationship candidates. The fact that they do not find that genuinely loving relationship indicates that there is another problem. Some blame it on the busy and fragmented lives they lead. Others point the finger at television, sports, and the image-obsessed institutions of society such as fashion and advertising. The wiser ones have grown weary of finger-pointing, and know that the real problem resides within.

Whether you are single, divorced, or even currently in an intimate relationship, you are probably tired of making the same relationship mistakes over and over again. Kathlyn and I feel a great deal of empathy for anyone in this situation, because we have been there ourselves. Before we found each other, we had begun to sink into that same kind of despair. We were afraid we would never attract the kind of love we really wanted. Until we discovered the tools and insights you will learn in this program, we would get out of one painful entanglement, only to find ourselves bogged down in a similar version of it a few days later.

Fortunately we found a way to make the changes necessary to move from the intense pain of unconscious relationships to twenty-plus years of the most blissful and creative relationship we could have imagined. In this program, we will show you exactly how to make those inner shifts yourself so that you can draw genuine, lasting love into your life. Kathlyn and I use everything you will learn in this book in our own relationship and, although we have been together for a long time now, every year has been richer and better than the one before because of what you will learn here.

What we discovered, in our own lives and through research with thousands of others, is that there are several principles and techniques that people must learn before they can create the kind of relationship that they truly desire. In fact, without realizing it at the time, Kathlyn and I used the very same principles to make important shifts in how we related to ourselves and others that became the foundation on which we created our own relationship. We had to learn those principles "the hard way," by making a lot of relationship mistakes in our twenties and early thirties. Once we figured out these principles and techniques, it only took a month to meet each other. That was over twenty years ago, and since then we have had the pleasure of teaching these skills to over twenty thousand people around the world. It has been very satisfying, because almost every day of our lives, we get letters and emails from people who have mastered these skills, and gone out and created a brand-new conscious relationship—one that satisfies their deepest desires for genuine love.

After all is said and done, it is really genuine love that makes all the difference in the quality of our lives. Without genuine love, human beings feel constant longing. In *Attracting Genuine Love*, we have created a program that gives very specific answers to the question, "How can I attract genuine love into my life?" It is a program that has been carefully refined in working with thousands of people over the past decade, and also includes nine guided practices on the enclosed CD that are the most powerful techniques we have found for creating the kind of real change in your life that will erase even a lifetime of unsatisfying relationships. If you follow these steps, you will discover what has been holding you back from getting the kind of love you really want and need. You will know exactly how to bring genuine love into your life, and how to keep it. ♥

CHAPTER
ONE

The Power of Commitment

HERE IS THE BOTTOM-LINE truth about how to begin the process of creating a conscious relationship: Nobody has the slightest chance of creating and sustaining a healthy relationship until they make a conscious commitment to it. Up until the moment you make a conscious commitment to attracting and keeping genuine love, your unconscious programming will run your love live (and usually ruin it). And once you make a conscious decision to change your unconscious programming, you have already taken the hardest step to attracting genuine love.

Whether you realize it or not, you are already demonstrating incredible power to create what you want—in fact, your current life is an example of the incredible power you possess to create, consciously or unconsciously. You may not like all that you have created. You might even refuse to accept that you have created your life through your choices, and believe instead that it is something that has been "done to you." It is true that you may not have consciously chosen many of the elements of your current life; nevertheless, it is your power that has manifested them. You were able to do this because of the power of commitment. The power of commitment has given you all the things that you now have.

TAKING FULL RESPONSIBILITY FOR THE CIRCUMSTANCES OF YOUR LIFE

In the late seventies, during an argument with my lover of five years, I suddenly realized that it was not our several-hundredth argument. It was our several-hundredth run-through of the same argument. A light bulb came on and a moment of awareness shined down upon me, and I clearly saw that our arguments always followed the same pattern of misery-producing moves.

I stepped back from the process and wondered, "Why would I engage in a pattern like this? Given all the experiences I could be having as a human being, why do I keep repeating the pattern of lying and being lied to, being criticized and criticizing, blaming and being blamed, thinking of myself as a victim?"

Then, in a rush of eye-opening realization, I got the answer: These things kept happening because I was committed to being criticized, committed to being betrayed, committed to arguing and lying. I was more committed to them than I was to being close. If I was lonely, it was because I was more committed to being lonely than I was to being connected. If I was overweight, it was because I was more committed to being overweight than I was to being slender. The moment I realized what my commitment was, I felt a shift.

I did not like this idea very much when I first realized it—in fact, it actually made me angry—but I soon discovered that I was surrounded by the results of my real commitments, and that the circumstances of my life were direct evidence of my real commitments.

It is important not to overestimate the level of your responsibility for the circumstances of your life. Although the present circumstances of your life are direct evidence of your real commitments, you certainly did not cause the situations of your birth, or diseases such as cancer or heart disease, or the global conditions of war and poverty. Taking responsibility for the present circumstances of your life in the sense I am using it can never be assigned, it can only be claimed, and the reason it is claimed is that taking responsibility for the circumstances of your life is the key to creating what you really want. Once you take responsibility for the circumstances of your life, you also release the energy you have tied up in old commitments of blame and resentment to fuel your commitment to a new kind of relationship.

Take a moment now to experience what it might be like to take full responsibility for the circumstances of your life. For just a moment, imagine that if you are lonely, it is because you are more committed to being lonely than you are to being connected. If you are overweight, it is because you are more committed to being overweight than you are to being slender. If you are unhappy with your job, it is because you are more committed to being unhappy in your job than you are to searching for a job that makes you happy. If you are unlucky in love, it is because on some level (usually unconscious) you are committed to being unlucky in love.

LISTEN TO TRACK 1
The Commitment
Meditation

The purpose of our first guided process—the Commitment Meditation—is to assist you in discovering your present level of commitment to attracting genuine love into your life.

UNCOVERING YOUR UNCONSCIOUS COMMITMENTS

We have talked about the power of conscious commitments and the power of getting clear on what you really want. Of equal power is your ability to reclaim and re channel the power of your unconscious commitments.

An unconscious commitment is an interpretation of reality that is often created in the first few years of life. Whatever we experience in our early years becomes very deeply ingrained in our personalities and we tend to seek out—or attempt to re-create—similar situations in our future relationships. This can be very problematic when our unconscious commitments concern aspects of relationship such as fear of abandonment or fear of being smothered.

It takes a lot of courage to acknowledge these unconscious commitments. It is much easier to blame everything on forces outside of us. When bad things happen to us repeatedly, it is even more tempting to blame outside forces. Some morning when your toaster sputters and dies, your car will not start, and the cat will not touch its food, it is much easier to think that it has something to do with the position of the planets than it is to take responsibility for the choice to buy that particular toaster, that model car, that brand of cat food. When life gets rough, our tendency to project the blame on outside forces gets even more pronounced. When bad things happen, it takes a leap of courage to acknowledge that we may be committed to those particular bad things happening. We close our eyes to the obvious truth, and then—lo and behold—we repeat the same patterns over again.

It is also much easier to complain than it is to explore our unconscious commitments. Do a quick scan of your lifetime of social interactions. How many complaints do you think you have uttered or heard? Probably thousands. Now, ask yourself how many times you have heard someone say, "Things are not going well for me. I am looking into how I may be sabotaging myself."

Usually those unconscious commitments come out of early life experiences, and in my case, my mother and several other important women in my family either distanced themselves from me, or actually left the family. This created an unconscious commitment in me to expect abandonment that I then used as a self-fulfilling prophecy in my close relationships.

Throughout my teens and twenties, I found myself in one relationship after another where there was emotional distance, betrayal, and abandonment. For a long time, I just complained that "women are all the same." After I saw the same patterns in half a dozen different relationships, I finally woke up and realized it was I who was "all the same." I realized I was committed to getting involved with women who were distant and who would eventually abandon me. Seeing that I created my painful dramas out of my unconscious commitments was a big wake-up moment for me.

Next I found myself wondering, "Why would I be committed to this kind of pain?" Where would the unconscious commitments be coming from that propelled me into these sickeningly repetitive soap operas? Immediately the answer came through from some part of me: I was engaged in this drama from the moment of my conception! The drama started before I did.

The drama of my conception involved my father's betrayal of my mother, and her shame and fury and hatred of her pregnancy (and lying about its very existence). In a sense, my existence ruined my mother's life, and I do not think she ever forgave herself, my father, and, by extension, me for getting her into the mess.

After my birth, my grandmother took charge of me while my mother went away to heal herself. Abandonment was written into my script almost before the curtain went up. In fact, all of the elements of the drama were there when I walked on stage. By the time I could think for myself (or even walk by myself), I had already been immersed in this drama for years.

This story has a happy ending, though—in fact, it was a major turning point in my life. I eventually realized that the whole thing was someone else's drama. It was not my problem! It was a problem between my mother and father. I had gotten caught up in it because I happened to be in the neighborhood. In that remarkable moment of clarity, I realized I did not need to take the problem personally, since it would have happened to anyone who happened to be in that particular womb at that time.

In this case, to take responsibility for my situation was a two-fold process. The first step was to take responsibility for my unhappy relationships—and the second part of the process was to realize that I had inherited elements from someone else's script, and that I could consciously choose a different script for the rest of my life.

Think about it: how many of your painful dramas actually started before your conception? If you look at each of them closely enough, you may find that a great many of them are really somebody else's drama. You just soaked them up by osmosis by being around them at an early age.

Take a moment and see if you can sense how much of the situation surrounding and preceding your birth determined your early and formative years. Can you see any patterns in your life—especially surrounding your romantic relationships—that seem to be more something you inherited rather than something you chose? Can you find any echoes of your parents' or even your grandparents' life themes in your romantic relationships?

At first this might seem at odds with the instructions to take responsibility for your life and your behaviors, but part of the process of untangling your unconscious patterns is first to become aware of them. In unconscious relationships, people often repeat the same patterns over and over again, week after week, year after year. In unconscious relationships, people do not talk about what is real, and they do not listen deeply to themselves or each other. In unconscious relationships, you do not feel appreciated, you do not know how to solve problems so they stay solved, and you cannot decide whether to stay or get out.

The great value of acknowledging that you have created your past love life out of your unconscious commitments is that you reclaim that energy and can direct it toward your conscious commitments. The moment you say, "I got where I am by my choices, most of which were driven by unconscious commitments," you free up the energy that was bound up in those old commitments and become free to make new conscious commitments.

But how do you go about finding out what your unconscious commitments are? You could do it through working with your dreams and many other techniques, but the fastest way is to examine your habitual complaints. What we have discovered in our work is that what people complain about in close relationships is often identical to their unconscious commitments. For example, say your number one complaint about your partner or partners in the past is that they were always criticizing you. If so, it is likely that you are unconsciously committed to bringing critical people into your life based on similar experiences you had while growing up.

Another common experience is that people come into a relationship with powerful unconscious commitments—such as being criticized—and their partners unconsciously pick up on the commitment and begin to act in ways that will supply what their partner is asking for unconsciously. I have had thousands of examples in couples counseling over the years where a person has said something like, "You know, I wasn't even a particularly critical person until I got into this relationship, and then suddenly I became a constant nag." What usually happens is that when we analyze their interactions and past histories, we find out that the other person has a commitment to being criticized that is so strong that it seemingly draws it out of their partner.

Sometimes it can be painful or difficult to look at and take responsibility for these aspects of ourselves. For example, I was once obese, and I struggled with that for a long time, but never was able to lose weight until I realized that I was unconsciously committed to being overweight. The moment I had that realization, I began to use all of the energy I had wasted in thinking I was the victim of my weight problem to lose weight and get more exercise. Within a year, I was no longer overweight.

Each time you catch yourself complaining about something, it is an opportunity to reclaim the power of one of your own unconscious commitments, and with it the opportunity to access its creative power for your own conscious purposes. It is also important to remember that this is a lifelong process. Even though I have been practicing it for over thirty years, hardly a week goes by that I do not hear myself complaining about something. But if I can catch myself in the act of complaining, I can turn it around and begin to wonder, "Why would I be unconsciously committed to that?"

I used this technique with a couple who came to me because they were unable to find a way to accommodate their different social styles. The husband was an extrovert and felt very comfortable at parties, whereas his wife was somewhat introverted and often felt uncomfortable and self-conscious, especially when he left her side to talk with others. This led to a lot of conflict in their relationship. She saw him as a flirt who abandoned her at parties, and he saw her as socially inept and unreasonably critical of him for enjoying himself in social situations.

The first thing I asked them to do was to take responsibility for creating their current relationship dynamic. He needed to be with a woman who was introverted and critical of him in social situations, and she had sought out a relationship with an extrovert who would abandon her at parties. At first they thought this was ridiculous—of course they would not choose to be in a relationship like this, because this was exactly the kind of behavior that was threatening their relationship! But as I got the wife to begin to verbalize her conscious commitment to a relationship with someone like her husband, she suddenly recalled that her father had also been an extrovert and flirt, and that this had caused a great deal of stress between her mother and father when she was a child. Her husband as well, in voicing his unconscious commitment to be with an introvert who was critical of his behavior in social situations, realized that these conflicts were also present between his own mother and father.

Once some of the excitement of this discovery had worn off, I watched their curiosity about each other intensify as they took the energy that they had been using to protect themselves and attack the other to consciously create practical solutions to accommodate and support each other in social situations in the future.

It is in the very act of wondering about why you might be unconsciously commit-ted to the things that you have been complaining about that the powerful work gets done. I highly recommend that you open up this wondering state of consciousness when you enquire into these things in your self, because you cannot find out what your unconscious commitments are if you are also feeling self-critical about them. In other words, you cannot beat your unconscious commitments out of yourself or criticize them out of yourself. What I have found is that they only bubble up to the surface when we are open-hearted and loving and accepting of ourselves, and can approach our unconscious commitments in a wondering state of mind and not a critical state of mind.

LISTEN TO TRACK 2
Uncovering Your Unconscious
Commitments

How do you find out what your unconscious commitments are? The guided process included as Track Two on the enclosed CD contains the fastest process we know for identifying, reclaiming, and re-channeling the power of your unconscious commitments. ♥

CHAPTER
TWO

Whole-Body Learning

ONE OF THE IRONIES of finding genuine love is that you first have to believe in it before you can find it. If you have never experienced it, or if all of your previous efforts have been frustrated or disappointed, there is probably a part of you that questions genuine love as a real possibility. This part of you that hopes, but does not believe, is often the part that prevents you from finding what you desire because, when you get close, it will be pulling in the opposite direction, afraid that you are being led astray by false hopes. Every time you hoped in the past, you got hurt, so why should this time be any different? And it probably will not be any different, at least not until you learn to bring all of you into agreement and focus on a clear objective—in this case, finding genuine love.

The best way we have learned to bring all of these pieces together is a process we call *Whole-Body Learning*. Whole-Body Learning is a means to harness the power of your conscious mind, your unconscious mind, and your *bodymind*. I use the word *bodymind* here to describe something that you will be experiencing in Whole-Body Learning: that although most of us would say that we experience our thoughts—and even our emotions—in our minds or brains, it will become clear that we also experience our emotions and feelings in our bodies, and that thoughts often have emotions associated with them, and vice versa. The physical experience of our thoughts, feelings, and emotions is what I will be referring to as our *bodymind*.

Whole-Body Learning practices are designed to create new programming for your bio-computer—this complex web of body, consciousness, and unconsciousness that we are. A great deal of your present experience is created by programming that was created when you were very young. Creating new programs and loading them into your bio-computer using these practices is the quickest and most permanent means we know to create real change, which is why we will be using guided Whole-Body Learning practices so extensively throughout this program.

You have probably had Whole-Body Learning experiences while learning how to drive a car or how to swim. While learning how to ride a bike, for instance, there was probably a moment when you suddenly "got it," and since then, you have always known how to ride a bike. Even if you do not get on a bike for thirty years, you will still have the Whole-Body Learning inside you.

One of the problems with books that focus on information and instruction is that your conscious mind is very useful for certain things, but it lacks the power by itself to quickly bring about deep and lasting behavioral change. For example, you might make up your mind to go on a diet or quit smoking or to get over an old lover, but unless you can get the agreement of your unconscious mind and your bodymind, you will probably find that your old habit patterns ultimately overpower your conscious mind.

Our goal in Whole-Body Learning is to align the thinking skills of your conscious mind with the power of your unconscious and your bodymind. Your unconscious mind is also very powerful, but it obviously needs the direction and the thinking skills of your conscious mind to harness its power in ways that can really serve you. For instance, if you consider yourself "accident prone" or "unlucky in love," there are probably self-perpetuating ideas that have been programmed into your unconscious that will get in your way when you decide to change your behavior.

What we will be calling the *bodymind* is that part of you which experiences sensations and feelings that cannot be considered as existing in either your conscious or unconscious mind. To understand the difference between thinking a concept in your conscious mind and feeling it in your body, think for a moment of the concept of *thirsty.* You could say "I am thirsty," but the experience of being thirsty is actually a dry sensation in your mouth and throat. You could even claim to be thirsty when your body was not actually experiencing thirst, but if you felt the sensation in your body, you would know for certain that it was true.

The following is a Whole-Body Learning technique that we will be using extensively to replace negative thought patterns with positive ones. In this and other written exercises, we encourage you to use a brand-new journal or notebook that you will dedicate to the exercises in this program. In this way, your notebook will become a journal of your path to finding genuine love.

The first step is to repeat the following sentence silently to yourself, replacing the blank with your name.

I, _____, consciously commit to doing whatever work is necessary to create lasting love in my life.

Once you have silently repeated the sentence to yourself, let your awareness sink into your body for about fifteen to twenty seconds, and see if you can experience some physical sensation related to this commitment. Do you feel a confidence surrounding it? Do you feel a nervousness, a doubt? At this point, it is not important what the sensations might be. Just become aware of them. Once you have completed this cycle, repeat it four to six times over a period of about two minutes—say the sentence silently to yourself, and then see if you can discover a physical sensation related to it in your body. Also note, as you repeat the exercise, if the physical sensations change over the course of the exercise.

Then take out your journal. (In this and other exercises where you will be asked to write, we have found that it is more effective if you do it in your own handwriting rather than typing it out.) Now, write the sentence in your journal, filling in the blank with your name. As you do this, notice any feelings that come up as you commit yourself to paper. Do you experience different sensations or the same sensations as when you were repeating this sentence silently to yourself? Does it bring it up fear? Sadness? Anger? Joy? Just notice what comes up in your body and conscious mind as you write out the sentence.

Now, do a sincerity check in yourself. Ask yourself: "Am I sincere about this commitment?" If your answer is no, there is absolutely nothing wrong with you. In fact, this is perhaps the most important information you could receive about why your past and present relationships are not working out—it is because you are not actually wholeheartedly open to the possibility of a lasting love relationship. If this is true for you, until you can actually go in and change your underlying expectations and make a commitment for what you desire, not only are your chances of finding it small, but the chances that your unconscious will sabotage any real possibility of attaining it are great as well.

What you need to do if your answer is "No" is to work through the following exercises in this program until you can successfully uncover the underlying causes for your inability to sincerely make this commitment. You can even use this exercise as a test as you proceed through this program—you can come back to it again and again and see how your feelings about this statement of commitment changes over time. Some day when you do your sincerity check, you will feel a resounding "Yes!" and when you do, you will be ready to rapidly progress to finding and developing a new, genuinely loving relationship.

Now, once you have completed your sincerity check, switch the pen or pencil to your non-dominant hand and write the sentence out again. (That is, if you wrote the sentence originally with your right hand, now write the sentence with your left hand.) Just scrawl it out as best you can—it does not have to be legible to anybody but you. Writing the commitment with your non-dominant hand is important, because your non-dominant hand is connected directly to your unconscious mind.

Now, switch back to your dominant hand and write it again. Then write it once more with your non-dominant hand. If you have done it as described, you should have two sentences written with your dominant hand and two written with your non-dominant hand.

When you finish this exercise and the other Whole-Body Learning exercises in this program, take a break. Go for a walk, perhaps, or get a bite to eat. These powerful exercises will continue working within you on a very deep level. Later, when you come back from your break, you can go on to the next section of this program, or save it for another day.

The Whole-Body Learning process is most effective if you continue to repeat the writing portion of each exercise on subsequent days to reinforce this reprogramming your bio-computer. You should write the sentence out again several more times, alternating your dominant and non-dominant hand, noticing any feelings (positive or negative) that arise in your bodymind as you do. And at the end of the process, do a sincerity check on yourself—see if you can sense a change in how sincere you are about your commitment.

THE BODY SCAN

Another way to utilize your bodymind is to explore your physical sensations around certain concepts. For instance, a good place to begin is to pause for a moment and get in touch with the feeling of love inside yourself. The experience of love is usually spiritual and mental as well as emotional and physical, but just for now, feel how you experience love in your body. Is it a warm, expanding sensation in your chest, or is it an open spaciousness in the center of your body? Everyone's experience is a little different, so tune in to what love feels like to you.

Next, get in touch with your experience of loving yourself. For some people, this might be quite a difficult step, and we will go into the process of learning to love yourself in greater depth later in this program, but for now, simply close your eyes and see if you can locate the feeling of loving yourself somewhere in your body. Also notice if "loving yourself" feels different or is located in a different place than the feeling of "loving other people." Over the next couple of weeks, return to this feeling of loving yourself as often as you like. Notice if your experience of loving yourself changes as you do it more often.

As you work through this program, it is important to let yourself feel all your feelings. It is natural and normal to have lots of feelings come up as you think about these crucial issues. The more you know about how you feel and what is going on in your body, the more success you will have. This may be challenging at times, but do the best you can, because these indicators will lead you to where you want to go, eventually leading you to what you most desire. The best way I know how to do that is with the *Body Scan*, a technique that enables you to tune into your physiological experience of emotions, which I will guide you through on Track Three of the enclosed CD. ♥

LISTEN TO TRACK 3
The Body Scan

CHAPTER
THREE

Learning How to Overcome Fear

TAKE A MOMENT right now and think about the things that are hardest to love about you. Is it your fear of being alone? Perhaps it is something you did in the past that is hardest for you to love. Examples of the kind of things people have written down in this exercise are "my weight," "the fact that I owe child support," "my addiction to drugs," "smoking cigarettes," etc. Write down as many of these qualities as you can in your notebook, as quickly as you can, without thinking about it too much, as follows:

The things that are the hardest for me to love about myself are: _____.

Looking at your list, you can probably imagine how difficult it would be for anyone with these qualities to find (or deserve) genuine love. That is why most of us spend our lives running from these unlovable parts of ourselves. When we finally confront it, we usually discover that it is a kind of fear.

For instance, in the early days of my relationship with Kathlyn, I can remember criticizing her for what I considered flirting at a party—for paying too much attention to others and not enough to me. But when I began to look closely at my reaction rather than her behavior, I realized that this feeling was a familiar one in my life, and its roots were actually in a fear of abandonment that I had developed in my first year of life. Once I realized my own responsibility for this feeling, I realized it had nothing to do with her, and once I understood the heart of the issue, I never again experienced this sense of abandonment, but until I directly confronted my underlying fear, I continued to experience this same reaction, and subsequently thought of myself as being flawed or unworthy of love.

The good news is that thinking of yourself as unworthy of love is just an idea that is only real if you believe it to be real, and then it is only real for you. And, since any idea is just a thought, and any thought can be replaced by a different thought, you can replace this feeling of being fundamentally flawed and unworthy of love with a feeling that, regardless of your past experiences, you can now take full responsibility for your life, and that you will use the power of this commitment to attract genuine love into your life. When you are able to accomplish this, you will not only feel differently about yourself, but other people will feel differently about you as well. In fact, in many ways, the journey of conscious loving is a process of bringing to the surface all of the fears and negatives that you believe stand between you and the experience of feeling loved, and then healing them.

One of the common fears many of us have to confront is the fear of abandonment. You can probably see how this fear will create havoc in your relationships. When you are afraid of being left alone, you will either keep people distant so it will not hurt so badly if they leave you; or you will leave first, before they have a chance to leave you; or you will dependently cling to them so they cannot leave you.

Another common fear is the dread of being smothered by another person. When you are in the grip of this fear, you are worried that your individuality and freedom will be lost if you surrender to full union with the other person, so you usually either stay at an arm's length—just as a person who is afraid of drowning might stand a yard or so away from the water's edge—or you leave them, emotionally or physically, at the moments when true intimacy is possible.

Another powerful fear is the one you discovered by making a list of your unlovable qualities—that we are "damaged goods" or that there is something fundamentally wrong or flawed deep inside us that makes us unworthy or unlucky in love and life.

For me, a certain fear—accompanied by anger and grief—was what I discovered was hardest for me to love about myself. After some unflinching self-inquiry, I came across a fear of abandonment that ran every destructive program I operated, from binge-eating to pushing away people who were trying to love me. Based on events in my first year of life, I was afraid of being left to die, and this fear gave rise to a host of other problems.

The two most troublesome behaviors were my eating disorder and my habit of pushing away love. I ate to quell my fear, and this habit made me a three-hundred-pounder by the time I was in my twenties. I also rejected people who were trying to help me—later I discovered that I pushed them away so they would not leave me. If I pushed them away, my crazy mind figured, I would be in control of who did the leaving.

That was a good day when I figured out the real truth: I am lovable even though I had some abandonment experiences in my early life. They do not need to affect how I live my life in the present.

Take a moment to ask yourself: Which of these fears feel familiar? Am I afraid of being abandoned? Am I afraid of being engulfed? Am I afraid that I am fundamentally flawed and unworthy of love? Do I have other fears as well?

In your notebook, write a list of your common fears around relationships. Try to see how these fears caused many of the problems in your prior relationships, and sabotaged many potential relationships. Can you see how, if you cannot heal these fears, you will continue to have similar problems in future relationships?

The reason we will continue to have difficulties in our relationships until we heal our fears is that, to keep our fears under control, we tend to keep people at a distance and push down the very aspects of ourselves that most need to come to the surface to be loved.

The good thing to know about fear is that it is simply a pulsating quiver of queasy sensations in your stomach area. In fact, the eminent psychiatrist Fritz Perls has described fear as "excitement without the breath." When you can consciously embrace and even learn to love your fears directly, you can actually feel them change or even disappear. Then in the space where the fear used to be, you will feel a big open space into which good things can enter, including the kind of relationship you desire.

One of the most important aspects of learning to attract and enjoy genuine love in your life is learning how to dissolve the fears and anxieties that have blocked you from feeling love in the past. The simple breathing technique I teach on Track Four is a way to turn those fears into excitement, using the simple natural resources of your breathing. ♥

LISTEN TO TRACK 4

Breathing into Fear

CHAPTER
FOUR

From Unlucky in Love to Lucky in Love

IF YOU ARE DOING THIS program, it is likely that you have at least occasionally thought of yourself as being unlucky in love, or feel an insecurity or awkwardness when meeting new people to whom you are attracted. It is important to release yourself from this limiting understanding, because you will need this energy to make a new commitment to being lucky in love.

Here is exactly how to find that "unlucky-in-love" part of you. You may be surprised how easy it is, but you may also be surprised at how powerful it is. Look at the following timeline:

YOUR UNLUCKY IN LOVE TIMELINE

Before I was born
Before I could walk
By the time I began school
When I was in elementary school
By the time I entered middle school
When I became aware of the opposite sex
When I began dating
When my first serious relationship ended
During high school
During college
When I began working for a living
At the time of my first marriage
When I became a parent
At the time of my divorce
When I first began dating after my divorce
When I first felt no longer young or attractive
At the time of my second divorce

Be sure to add any other significant moments from your own life to the above timeline.

Close your eyes for a moment and try to tune in to your feeling of awkwardness when you meet new people or of "being unlucky in love." It might be a vague body feeling, or maybe it is a thought in your mind. Somewhere in you, though, you can sense the part of you that feels unlucky. Just give it some attention for a moment.

Now, with one of your fingers, point to the place on the timeline where you first became aware of feeling awkward or being unlucky in love. There is probably no way to know for sure, of course, but just accept whatever answers you get from inside yourself. For example, if you have always felt unlucky, you would probably point to "Before I was born." If you started feeling unlucky when you were in high school, point to that part of the timeline. Do not go further until you have identified one or more of the points on the timeline.

Now, think for a moment about your parents and your grandparents. Most of us who feel awkward meeting people come from either parents or grandparents who felt that way, too. By being around them, we picked up their attitudes unconsciously. (If you were adopted, think of your birth-parents as well as your adoptive parents. If you never knew your grandparents, think of any stories you have heard about them.)

My mother
My father
My mother's parents
My father's parents

Now, with one of your fingers, point at any or all of your parents and grandparents as listed above if you feel they were unlucky in love. There is no way you can know for sure—just go with your impression if you feel they were unlucky. If you do not at first feel they were unlucky, try waiting a moment and see if you can get any feelings of anything that would suggest they camouflaged their unhappiness as something else—perhaps in a perceived sense of victimhood, chemical dependence, or chronic illness.

BREAKING THE GRIP OF THE PAST

Now, I would like you to use the power of Whole-Body Learning to do something incredibly important for changing your luck in love.

Look at the timeline again. Point with your finger to a place on it when you felt unlucky. Now, as you say the following sentence, point at the timeline while you say out loud, "That was then"—and then touch your chest with that same finger as you say "This is now." Do this at least ten times. It is important that you physically touch your chest when you say "This is now," and make sure that you say it out loud. Do this a minimum of ten times, but you can do it dozens of times if it feels right to you to do so.

Then, we would like you to do something similar with your parents and grandparents. If you feel that your parents or grandparents were unlucky, point to them as you say "That was them," and touch your chest with that same finger as you say "This is me." Do this at least ten times.

After you finish doing this, take a break. Come back later or another day for the next session. ♥

CHAPTER
FIVE

Loving Yourself Unconditionally

THE MAJOR BARRIER to a loving relationship is an unloved and unaccepted part of ourselves that keeps us from forming and keeping genuine love. Most of us have aspects of ourselves that we have never loved and accepted, which causes us to run around in desperation, trying to get someone else to love us. Our hope is that, if they give us enough love, our unlovable part will go away, but it never does, because people who do not love themselves attract other people who do not love themselves. Then they try to get the other person to love them unconditionally, but another person's love, no matter how powerful or unconditional, can never substitute for the experience of loving ourselves. Yet the moment you love the unloved parts of yourself unconditionally, you dissolve the biggest barrier to receiving and giving genuine love. In addition, when you love yourself deeply and unconditionally for everything you are and everything you are not, you attract people who love and accept themselves, just as when you feel fundamentally unlovable deep down inside yourself, you will attract people who feel the same way about themselves.

Take out your notebook and look at the list you made of everything you find hard to accept about yourself. Go through the list and focus on each entry individually for a few seconds in a spirit of loving acceptance. Love these qualities deeply in yourself, so you will not require anyone to love them for you.

If you can learn to accept and love each of your "weaknesses" or "personal failings" with your whole heart, you will no longer try to get others to love those aspects for you. If you can accept and love each of these qualities completely, you will no longer keep running from them. Plus, if you can learn to accept and love these aspects of your self, you can free up all of the energy you have been using to either cover up or to compensate for your perceived flaws.

If you have trouble feeling complete and total acceptance of these qualities, you can try a technique we use with our clients. First, think of what day of the week it is. If it is Thursday, you can accept that without difficulty. Now, see if you can transfer that same matter-of-fact acceptance to the qualities you feel make you unlovable.

The way it worked for me is that when I finally gave myself that split second of unconditional love, I felt free for the first time in my life. How liberating it was to love myself for something that had moments before been unthinkably unlovable! Now, I cheerfully admitted the obvious: I am a fat person who pushes away love!

But it was not the kind of slogan I wanted chiseled on my tombstone! So, I radically rewrote my life-script. I went on a diet: for a year, I ate foods I had never touched before ... mostly fruits and vegetables. I lost one hundred pounds in twelve months, and felt fabulous.

I also put myself on a different sort of diet, one that was much harder to stay on: I quit pushing away love. I accepted help. I told people my feelings. I quit pretending that I knew everything. As if by magic, a world of love opened up before me. Soon I was surrounded by love, completely encircled by it. It had been there all the time, waiting for me to let it in.

As I loved myself, I suddenly found myself making another shift of consciousness. Up until that moment, I had always felt slightly disconnected from other people and the world around me, even though I had not been aware of feeling that way. I was disconnected and did not know it—I thought that was just the way everybody felt. Disconnection was the way life was. Suddenly a shift occurred deep within me, and I felt connected to other people and to the world around me. A wall disappeared ... one I had not even known I was hiding behind.

It was also a physical shift that I could feel. I can compare the feeling of disconnection to having a tiny rock in my shoe. I had walked so long with the irritation that I had lost consciousness that I was irritated. Suddenly the rock was removed and, for the first time in memory, I took a step without irritation.

That is what loving ourselves can do. It frees us to walk through the world feeling at one with ourselves and other people. It is a new way to be, a way of being that makes every step of the journey richer and more delightful.

You may have to remind yourself that complete and unconditional self-acceptance has nothing to do with egotism or self-flattery. Egotistical people are desperately trying to get other people to love them, even though they feel deeply unlovable inside. That is why egotism and boasting make us so uncomfortable: we can sense that there is something insincere about it. But here we are talking about a genuine, sincere, heartfelt, and humble love for yourself. It is a feeling of accepting yourself for everything you are and everything you are not.

Kathlyn and I have never met anyone who loved themselves deeply and unconditionally all of the time. You can, however, make a commitment to experiencing self-acceptance in a healthy way. One way to begin is to make a commitment to loving yourself—even for a second or two—and work up from there. That way, you will have the experience of self-love to fall back on when you find yourself in the grip of your unlovable part. And, by awakening the flow of unconditional love inside yourself, you open a space for an unconditional lover to come into your life as well.

Unconditional self-acceptance is a process that takes practice. The meditation included as Track Five in this program is an opportunity to learn to love yourself unconditionally—not as a concept, but as an actual living experience. ♥

LISTEN TO TRACK 5
Learning to Love
Yourself Meditation

CHAPTER
SIX

A Soul-Shifting Commitment

ONCE YOU HAVE MADE a commitment to loving yourself unconditionally, and accepted that it is okay to desire a committed relationship, the next step necessary to attract a new kind of relationship into your life is to make a commitment to it, as well. In fact, nothing else but a soul-level commitment will do. Unless you are certain that this is what you truly want—and that nothing else will do—you will find yourself sabotaging any potential relationships as they appear.

I cannot overestimate the importance of this step, or the difficult self-questioning that is necessary before you can proceed. Since you bought this program and have read this far, it is safe to assume that you are interested not only in creating an authentic love relationship in your life, but that your past experiences have not satisfied that desire, and that you are ready to ask for help.

Now it is time for you to search your heart for the answers to two important questions: The first is "Do I really want to attract a genuine, conscious, and loving relationship into my life?" Stop and listen to your heart and soul when you ask yourself this question. If just asking this question makes you feel scared, nervous, or confused, you can imagine the kind of confusion you will experience when the possibility of a real relationship presents itself to you. But it is also important to accept—and even love—this uncertainty and fear as a part of your mental and emotional make-up. If just asking this question makes you experience fear, you can also go back to Track Four and practice breathing into your fear until you contact the excitement underneath. In fact, the intensity of the fear you experience around this self-questioning is often a measure of how deep your longing—and excitement—is for what you currently experience as fear.

It is also important to be aware that there is nothing wrong with you if your answer to this question is not a complete and total "Yes," but just know that until it is, you will probably continue to experience the same difficulties in relationships that you have experienced in the past. Doing these practices and learning some of the techniques and skills taught in this program will certainly bring you closer to a genuine loving relationship, but you will probably never fully experience the love you desire until your answer to this question is a complete and total "Yes"—on the level of your mind, heart, body, and spirit.

If you can ask yourself the question, "Do I really want to attract a genuine, conscious, loving relationship into my life?" and every part of you answers "Yes," then it is time to ask yourself another question: "Am I ready and willing to make a total commitment to something completely new in order to bring a conscious loving relationship into my life?"

You probably already know that what you have tried in the past has not worked, and that your only hope is to learn something new. It is also important to acknowledge that it is very difficult to commit to something new, especially since we have often tried new things in the past that have not worked out as we had originally hoped.

If the answer to the question "Am I ready and willing to make a total commitment to something completely new in order to bring a conscious loving relationship into my life?" is "No," it is important to embrace and love that resistance in yourself. Know that you have reasons for being distrustful, and that these reasons are based on your previous experiences. There is nothing wrong with learning from your past behavior to be distrustful of new experiences. It is also important to realize that until you can fully commit to trying something new, you will probably not be able to replace the kind of experiences that reinforce your distrust with the kind of new experiences that will lead to the relationship you most desire.

However, if your answer to this question is a complete and total "Yes," you should take a moment to congratulate yourself. Your willingness to take this next step is what will bring you what you most desire. Celebrate this "Yes" by using the Whole-Body Learning technique with the following sentence:

Yes, I am ready and willing to make a total commitment to something completely new in order to bring a conscious loving relationship into my life.

Repeat it in your mind until you can feel it in your body. Then, to cement your commitment, write it down in your journal with your dominant and non-dominant hands as a contract with yourself, and then do a sincerity check: how comfortable are you with this commitment?

When you can feel this commitment on a level beyond words, you will have all of the pieces in place to move forward with the next important step in the process, which is to go public with your commitment.

GOING PUBLIC WITH YOUR COMMITMENTS

Once you have aligned your mind, your expectations, and your body to your commitment to a conscious, loving relationship, it is time to go public with your commitment. By going public with your commitment to attracting genuine love, you give your journey tremendous power and focus—the kind of power and focus that you will need to reach your goal. The way you begin this part of the process is to say to someone you know, "I have made a commitment to attracting genuine love into my life."

When you make your announcement, you should also check in to see how you feel when making your commitment public. Any reservations you feel while making this announcement to a friend or acquaintance will tell you even more about how you feel about it on a "gut" or soul level. Do you say it with confidence, with surety? Do you feel that you are speaking one of your core truths? When you make this statement do you sense that you are breaking with your past and beginning a new process that will bring a new kind of love relationship into your life? Or is there any lingering doubt, insecurity, wavering, uncertainty, embarrassment, waffling, insincerity, or lack of confidence in your voice? Does it feel inauthentic; does your voice sound weak or hollow? Do you feel embarrassed or try to make a joke out of it? Do you believe yourself?

None of these responses are wrong or anything to feel guilty about. Your responses are indications of your true feelings, and by now, you probably know that unless you can get your body, conscious mind, and unconscious mind into alignment, you cannot possibly get (or keep) what you believe you want. Any ambivalence, fear, uncertainty, or insecurity exhibited when merely voicing your desire and intention will be experienced manifold by anyone with whom you begin a relationship.

But it is important that you do not take back your stated intention if you feel that there is any uncertainty in your voice. Rather, this is an indication of where you still have work to do. Go back and redo the earlier exercises and continue to practice speaking your commitment aloud. One day you will tell someone that you have made a commitment to bring genuine love into your life, and you will announce it with confidence.

When you make your announcement, you should also notice how the person you are confiding in responds. A statement such as "I am committed to attracting genuine love into my life" will often trigger strong responses in others, including bringing up all of their fears, disappointments, and hopes. This is not really surprising, as love is a very loaded subject for everyone. Perhaps they will feel inspired to declare the same thing for themselves. Maybe it will make them envious or sarcastic. Maybe it will stir up their despair. Maybe you will recognize some of their resistance, questioning, and doubts. How you handle their reactions can tell you whether you are sincere about your own commitment.

For example, suppose you tell a family member about your commitment and the person says, "You! You will never have a healthy relationship if you live to be a hundred! Nobody in our family has ever had ten seconds of genuine love! Who the heck do you think you are, anyway?" Or maybe they will laugh in your face, or become embarrassed by your announcement. In situations like this, it is best to be sensitive to their reactions, but do not feel a need to respond to or answer them. Ultimately, their reaction to your statement is really none of your business. Your business—as you have just told them—is attracting genuine love. If you are not sincere about your commitment, you may try to explain yourself to the person, quit the course, or make some other move that sabotages your commitment, but if you are sincere about your commitment to finding genuine love, you can just take a deep breath, smile, and realize you have no control over what other people think about you.

To aid you in this important step on the way to bringing genuine love into your life, we have created a special guided session included as Track Six on the enclosed CD. This practice will make use of a mirror, so have one at hand when you begin this session.

Once you have listened to Track Six, go out and tell at least one person of your commitment to bringing genuine love into your life. If it feels right, continue to tell more and more people of your commitment before you go on to the next chapter, when you will begin to design this genuine love relationship that you are now committed to discovering. ♥

LISTEN TO TRACK 6
Going Public with
Your Commitment

CHAPTER
SEVEN

Designing Your Next Relationship

THE IMPORTANCE OF DESIRE

Many of us, as we were growing up, were made to feel guilty and ashamed about wanting things. We may have been called selfish or impractical or unreasonable. That is exactly where Kathlyn and I found ourselves, in our late twenties and early thirties, when we first began to wake up from our long trance of unconscious relationships. We both realized, even before we met each other, that we felt guilty for wanting the kind of relationship we really wanted. And yet we also knew that unless we learned to ask for what we wanted, we had little chance of actually getting it.

You too may have felt guilty for having a desire for a specific kind of relationship, and the guilt may have caused you to submerge your desire. If that is true for you, write in your notebook: "I feel guilty for wanting a genuinely loving relationship." After you have written it down, stare at it the same way you did when looking at your list of unlovable qualities, and allow yourself to feel the depth of your guilt around your desire for a satisfying love relationship.

Now take a moment to love yourself for feeling guilty. Realize that it is natural and normal to feel guilty about desiring the kind of relationship you really want. After all, how much encouragement did you get for clarifying what you really want in a close relationship? How much encouragement did you ever receive for holding out for your highest desires?

I know that, personally, I did not get very much encouragement in this regard. In fact, until I was able to create the kind of relationship I have with Kathlyn, a part of me was afraid that I was doomed to miss out on life's big prize. Desperately wanting a total and fulfilling love relationship was a guilty secret that I buried inside myself. It was only when I finally consciously voiced my deepest desire that I was able to consciously receive and enjoy its fulfillment. Kathlyn's own story illustrates how difficult it can be to get support for going after our highest ideals:

"After a year of disappointment, heartbreak, and abuse, I decided to leave my first marriage. Since I was in my early twenties, I figured it was better to get out quickly and get on with the rest of my life, rather than waste my time hoping for something better to happen. Maybe I would find the right person, maybe I would not, but at least I would not be settling for less than I wanted. But when I told my mother about my decision, she gave me the exact opposite counsel. 'Stay put,' she told me, 'Even though it may be awful now, it could improve. And, you know, you could do a lot worse.' I did not see how I could do much worse, though, so I went ahead with my decision. It felt like I would be selling myself out if I stayed—any loneliness and hardship I might face by leaving seemed so much easier to deal with than the soul-shrinking feeling of settling for less."

It is important to admit to yourself that you really want a genuinely conscious, loving relationship. If you are like most of us, you know deep down in your heart that you will never feel fulfilled until you have one, and yet you have probably never stopped and admitted this truth to yourself. If this is really your heart's desire, it is not only okay to let yourself want this kind of relationship, it is essential to make the fulfillment of this desire one of your highest priorities. In addition, it is not until we allow ourselves to consciously desire something that we can consciously receive and enjoy it when it arrives.

You can begin this same process by using the Whole-Body Learning technique with the following sentence:

I want a genuine, conscious, loving relationship, and I will do whatever work on myself I need to do to make that desire come true.

Repeat it silently to yourself and try to feel it in your body. When you can do this, get out your notebook and write it out twice with your dominant, and then your non-dominant hand. Then do a sincerity check—how comfortable are you with this commitment?

When you have finished this process, take a break. Let the Whole-Body Learning technique continue to work on coordinating your conscious mind, your unconscious mind, and your bodymind with your willingness to continue the personal work necessary to bring a genuine, conscious, loving relationship into your life.

YOUR THREE ABSOLUTE NO'S

Now that you have made a commitment to attracting genuine love into your life, learned the importance of your unconscious commitments and the necessity of new conscious commitments, realized the importance of loving yourself unconditionally before anyone else can love you, and made your commitment public, now what? Having laid the foundation for a successful search, how can you begin the process of attracting genuine love?

Well, now that you have realized that many of your past experiences were based on unconscious commitments and early programming, the first thing to do is to uncover the qualities of these unsuccessful relationships so that you will be able to avoid them in the future.

Most of us are generally aware of what qualities caused us problems in our previous relationships. If we truly want something new in our lives, our next commitment should be not to get involved with people who demonstrate qualities that we are sure we do not want to reexperience in our next relationship. If you are clear about what you do not want in your life, you will more likely avoid repeating the same mistakes.

One way to discover an *Absolute No* is to look for the behavior in other people that has caused you the most intense pain in your relationships. For example, an alarmingly high percentage of abused women get out of one abusive relationship only to form another relationship with an abuser. Similarly, it is common for those who grew up in an alcoholic family to subsequently get involved with substance abusers.

In forming your Absolute No's, it is also useful to become aware of several of the common personality types, some of which you will want to avoid if you want to find the kind of relationship you desire.

One of the most useful categorizations of personality types I know was created by the gifted therapist Virginia Satir based on her experiences with thousands of families. Satir roughly divided people into five groups: *Blamers, Placaters, Super-Reasonables, Distracters,* and *Levelers*. Of course, some people are combinations of two or more of the above.

Blamers think you are responsible for their pain, and will not take any responsibility for the pain they create. They believe that the one who finds the most fault wins. You cannot win with a Blamer, and as a result, they make for a difficult relationship partner.

Placaters are always looking to please, but it is a desire to please that is based on fear. They are afraid of disapproval, so they do whatever they can to avoid it. Usually they sacrifice their relationship with themselves in the service of pleasing others, then they gradually develop a deep resentment about the sacrifice they are being "asked" to make—not realizing it is they themselves who have created the situations that are causing themselves so much pain and suffering. They make for difficult relationship partners because you never know for sure who they are or what they are feeling, and neither do they.

Super-Reasonables are cut off from their feelings and dismiss or even ridicule emotions, and believe that logic is the only way to operate. They are convinced that they are right about most things, and they spend a lot of their time trying to convince you of their authority and superiority. They are difficult to be in relationship with because they not only dismiss their own feelings and emotions, but will insist on dismissing yours as well.

Distracters are always changing the subject and creating uproars. If they cannot win, they will mess up the game so nobody else can win either. They believe the person who creates the biggest drama wins, regardless of what gets lost in the process. They are difficult to maintain a relationship with because life is constant chaos in their presence.

Levelers will tell you what is going on with them in a straightforward way, and they will listen to you compassionately if you level with them. They are easy to be around because they know that when people level with each other, their natural love and goodness will come forth. They know that having a good time and helping others have a good time is what life is all about. Every moment, they get the same choice everybody else does—the choice between love and creating melodramas based on fear—and they choose love.

I can give you a personal example of what taking an inventory of your previous relationships can be like. In 1979, I said "No" to ever again being in a relationship with someone with an active addiction. If the person used any tobacco, alcohol, or other drugs on a regular basis, I did not want to have a close relationship with them, because I had been in those kinds of relationship before, and I did not want to repeat those patterns. Apparently I meant it, because I have never had another close relationship with an addict.

My mother died from a drug addiction, and her addiction made my childhood chaotic. She practiced her addiction throughout her pregnancy with me, so I was literally in relationship with an addict from the moment of my conception. Based on this programming, in my early twenties I met, got involved with, and married an alcoholic. Amazingly, I was so oblivious that I never noticed that my spouse was an alcoholic until many years later. Then, after going through great pain and suffering in our divorce four years later, I immediately got involved with a woman who was addicted to tobacco, alcohol, and Valium. Once again, I was not even aware that she was an alcoholic or drug-dependent until a year into our relationship.

As I sat there on my floor in 1979, aged thirty-four, I counted up the significant relationships of my adult life. My scorecard (using Virginia Satir's personality types) looked like this: 3 Blamers, 1 Super-Reasonable, 1 Distracter, 2 Combo Platters, 1 Leveler.

Unfortunately for me (but to her great credit), my one Leveler had spent a frustrating couple of years with me, and then dropped me like a hot potato.

My scorecard revealed that I had a bad habit of attracting Blamers. I decided to say "No" to that pattern. I committed to being unwaveringly vigilant for any Blamers who strayed into my path.

So my first Absolute No was to say "No" to entering any relationship with a person who has an active addiction. My second Absolute No was not to get involved with anyone who was a Blamer—someone who blamed others for the circumstances of their life. My third Absolute No was never again to form a relationship with a category I call *Shirkers*. Shirkers are people who do not like to do their share of the work, whatever it is. I had learned the hard way that everybody fundamentally wears one of two T-shirts. One T-shirt has "What Can I Get?" written on the front, and the other has "What Can I Do to Help?" I seemed to attract people who proudly wore a "What Can I Get?" shirt, and then I would waste my energy complaining about having to do all the work. But who was the sucker who kept inviting these people into his life in the first place?

Now it is your turn to declare what kind of future you do not want for yourself. First, what is the most important quality that you do not want to invite into your life again? Write it down in your notebook.

The most important thing I vow never to invite into my life again is _____.
Then continue until you complete your list.
The second most important thing I vow never to invite into my life again is _____.
The third most important thing I vow never to invite into my life again is _____.

Are you clear on your three absolute No's? If so, great. If not, do some more reflecting on what you want to keep out of your love life. If your list has more than three qualities, see if you can choose the three most important qualities that you do not want to reexperience in your next relationship.

It is important to mention here that many people find it very difficult and painful to go back over their past relationships and take responsibility for having brought pain into their lives. Ultimately we have to accept our responsibility for the failures of our past relationships before we can forgive ourselves and accept what we have created in the past in order to move forward. Obsessing about the past consumes precious energy. We need to reclaim all that energy to have a full tank for our new relationship journey.

It is also important that we use this process to investigate any negative qualities that we brought into past situations, as well. Check your list of Absolute No's. Do you embody any of the qualities you do not want others to have? If so, you are setting yourself up for disappointment. If you do not want to be with someone who is addicted to chemicals, check to see if you have any chemical addictions yourself. If you do not want to be with a Blamer, make sure you are not a Blamer yourself. Be honest with yourself and see whether you need to do some personal work on your three Absolute No's. In many cases, this self-evaluation can be one of the most important parts of the process that will bring about the deep change that is necessary to begin a new—and satisfying—kind of relationship.

YOUR THREE ABSOLUTE YES'S

Now that you are aware of which qualities you do not want to invite into your next relationship, you can get clear on what qualities you would like to experience in your next relationship.

In 1979, back when I was sitting on the floor of my apartment, looking back over my life and my previous relationships, I decided that, if I wanted to have a new kind of relationship—a relationship that broke with the patterns of my past—I had to decide what qualities this new kind of relationship would have to possess.

I realized that the absolute most important thing to me was honesty. I did not want to spend another minute of my life concealing things from myself or anybody else. I did not want to spend another minute being with someone who was concealing something from me. I wanted to make sure I never had another conversation that went like this:

Me: What's going on? You look upset.
Other person: No, I'm just fine.

Invariably in these situations, three hours later, the truth would come out about what the person was upset about all along. This was also a conversation that went on with various members of my original family on hundreds of occasions. In this way, I had internalized the need for it so thoroughly that it is not surprising that I looked for—and found—women with whom I could simply transfer over this patterned behavior.

I decided to eliminate this sort of conversation from my life, and the way I decided to go about it was to make such a strong commitment to honesty that it would form something of a force field around me, which repelled dishonest people and invited only honest ones in. I said to the universe: "I commit to a relationship with a woman who is totally honest. I commit myself to unflinching honesty with myself and others, and I commit to inviting only honest people into my life." That was my first Absolute Yes.

My second Absolute Yes was: "I commit to a relationship with a woman who takes total responsibility for her life, her feelings, and what happens to her, in the way that I commit to taking total responsibility for my own life, my feelings, and what happens to me."

My third Absolute Yes: "I commit to a relationship with a woman who has her own creative path, and one that is harmonious with mine."

This commitment was important to me because I had struggled in past relationships with partners who were envious of my commitment to my creative path. My first wife was not a reader, for example, and often criticized me for spending time reading. In my life, though, sitting around reading is not a luxury—it is a fundamental requirement for my well-being. Another lover was jealous of the success of my first book. After feeling victimized by this, I finally woke up and took responsibility for creating this situation: I realized that if I were thoroughly committed to my own creativity, I would not create resistance to it. Resistance was simply evidence of my internal resistance to fully embracing my own creative life.

Now this is your opportunity to spend some time creating your own list of the three things you most want in a partner. First, what is the most important thing that you require in a relationship? What do you want to celebrate every moment of every day? Write it down in your notebook.

The most important thing I require and want to celebrate in a relationship is _____.
What is your second Absolute Yes?
The second most important thing I require and want to celebrate in a relationship is _____.
Now, what is the third most important quality you want in your relationship?
The third most important thing I require and want to celebrate in a relationship is _____.

Feel free to come up with a list that has more than three qualities, but once you have completed your list, see if you can choose from it the three most essential qualities that you want in your relationship. This process can help you to get further clarity on what is most essential to you.

The most important aspect of finding what you want in others is to first embody it yourself. Just as one of the biggest stumbling blocks in most relationships is that we seek in others what we cannot supply for ourselves—such as looking for someone to love us when we cannot love ourselves—the opposite is also true: if you embody the qualities you are looking for in a love partner, then you will find it easier to attract a love partner with those qualities.

So, take a moment and honestly look to see whether you have in yourself those qualities you most want in your love partner. If you are looking for honesty, are you impeccably honest? If dependability is one of your Absolute Yes's, are you dependable yourself? Be frank with yourself. If you find yourself coming up short on some of the qualities you are seeking in a love partner, you are setting yourself up for disappointment. Like attracts like, so focus on first becoming the person you want to attract. ♥

CHAPTER EIGHT

Real-World Rule Number One: Be Real

RULES THAT RUN THE UNIVERSE

The universe works according to certain principles, and life works best when we follow those principles carefully. The principle of gravity is one of those rules, and like most of these rules, once you learn how it works, you can avoid a lot of the pain and difficulty that comes from not understanding, or ignoring, it. Additionally, rapid change begins to happen in our lives when we learn not only how these rules work, but how to make them work for us.

From thirty years of working with people, and from twenty years of living and loving in a conscious relationship, I have discovered four key rules or principles that are critical for maintaining a positive loving relationship. It is important to understand and practice these four rules, because I can tell you from painful experience that you will blow any chances of a genuine loving relationship by breaking any of them. The good news is that these rules of relationship are as simple and as unavoidable as gravity. Once you learn how they operate, you can avoid a lot of the pain and difficulty you have experienced thus far in your relationships. And if you follow these principles, you get to live with a flow of well-being coursing through your body, a feeling of connection with the loving people around you, and a direct pipeline to the creative forces of the universe.

THE NUMBER ONE RULE OF CONSCIOUS RELATIONSHIPS: BE REAL

If you tell the truth at all times, you will have clear relationships with everyone. If you do not, things will get out of control very quickly. To get back into the flow of harmony, all you have to do is look to see where you stopped telling the truth to yourself or someone else, and fix it by telling the truth.

In other words, if you are driving down the highway and your car starts shimmying, look for the wheel that is out of alignment, and straighten it out. It does not take much of a misalignment to begin to shimmy, especially if you are whizzing along at a rapid clip. Many people, though, make the mistake of dealing with the shimmy by turning up the radio, in hopes that the passengers will not notice the real problem. Sometimes it works for a while, but eventually the truth comes out.

So, if your life stops working, look for a simple truth you "forgot" to tell. Sometimes it is a truth you are trying to hide from yourself, and sometimes it is one you are trying to hide from others. If you look underneath any major mess in anyone's life, you will usually find a truth that did not get told.

Almost everybody has a few things they have not come clean about—things that would restore integrity to their lives if they owned up to them. Most of the truths that we need to tell are simple truths, but getting to the simple truth is not always simple. The first step to begin this healing process is to make a commitment to being absolutely honest with yourself and everyone around you. Begin by cultivating the skill of saying simple but authentic things like "I am sad" and "I am angry" and "I would rather not do that."

In conscious relationships, absolute authenticity is required. If you do not tell the truth, you forfeit your right to genuine love. If you have had difficulty in maintaining your authenticity in your previous relationships, it is especially important that you begin practicing complete honesty right now. Then, when you meet someone you are interested in, you will have developed a habit of honesty that will become the means of meeting and connecting with that person on a genuine level. If they return your interest, you will feel that you are being responded to and respected for who you really are, rather than who you think they want you to be. In this way, you will not only feel better about yourself, but the interactions you have with your partner will be ones that reflect and grow out of your authentic self.

If maintaining complete honesty has been a problem for you in the past, one of the best ways to begin the process of becoming authentic is to look back over your life and see if you can find patterns that reveal something of your perceived need to be dishonest with yourself and others.

Take out your notebook and make a list of subjects or situations where you traditionally have had difficulty maintaining honesty. What is something that you have not told the truth about in your life? What is something that you have difficulty speaking about authentically with others? Any consistent themes usually indicate areas in which you feel embarrassment or shame. These are often areas that need your unconditional love and acceptance. As we did in Chapter Three, make a list of these problem areas and see if you can accept and love them unconditionally. With acceptance, these areas will loosen their power over your behavior and lessen your need to overcompensate for them by being less than totally honest.

An extra benefit to this process of becoming completely honest is that many of the areas that we feel the need to overcompensate for or to hide from others are the very kinds of admissions that bring us closer to others. We usually find that our unconscious fears are unfounded and, perhaps most surprisingly of all, shared by others as well. ♥

CHAPTER
NINE

Real-World Rule Number Two: Lead With Appreciation

IF YOU GO THROUGH life in a conscious state of appreciation, you will create a field of positive energy around you wherever you go. In fact, one of the most powerful means to change your daily life is to lead with appreciation. Leading with appreciation is very simple. All you have to do is start your conversations with a moment of genuine and conscious appreciation. For instance, if you go to the door to pay the person who delivers your paper, take a moment to realize how much you appreciate having your paper delivered to your house every day. When you can actually feel appreciation in your body and mind, say something like, "Thank you for bringing the paper every day," but have the words come out of your heart without much thought. Your sincerity is more important than the specific words you choose to say.

Leading with appreciation is especially important in your closest relationships, where the quality of your interactions often determine your satisfaction within the relationship. When you are not feeling appreciative, you are constantly on the lookout to be filled up by your partner. This not only creates tension and insecurity in your relationship, but also a kind of grasping that often actually pushes your partner away. If you are primarily a consumer in your relationship, you are operating out of a deficit mentality, and nothing the other person does can possibly be enough to fill you up.

But if you cultivate the expression of appreciation within your relationship, you essentially become not a consumer, but a producer. In addition, when you are not waiting around for people to appreciate you, you have more mental clarity with which to appreciate others. Once you are no longer operating out of this sense of scarcity, you also begin to think more positively and operate out of a sense of abundance, which in turn will attract a new kind of relationship into your life—a relationship that is different from the kinds of relationships that are manifested out of unconscious programming. When you begin to focus on others and express appreciation for them, you are also more likely to find yourself in a reciprocal flow of positive energy with other people.

This rule about appreciation has two stages. The first is to become conscious of something in your life that you value and appreciate. Secondly, by expressing it to others, you acknowledge not only that there is something admirable in them, but also that you are appreciative of it and them.

Just about any appreciation will do to get the flow of good feeling going. As you are walking down the street with a friend, you might notice the sunlight glinting on the fresh dew. In that moment, open your mouth and say, "Right now, I am appreciating the sunlight glinting on the dew." A simple noticing like this is often all it takes to put you in the flow of appreciation.

As you go through your day, notice what you notice. Then bring your appreciation of what you are seeing into your consciousness, and become aware not only of what you are appreciating, but of the feeling that surrounds the appreciation as well. And then, to complete the process, put your appreciation into words and express your appreciation out loud—to yourself or someone else.

I usually suggest that you try to speak a ten-second appreciation every hour. One day, in one of our workshops, a very tense and hostile-looking person took the microphone after I made that suggestion and said sarcastically, "So we are supposed to go around gushing all over the furniture all the time?" I had to laugh, as did most of the audience, but if a person thinks that saying one ten-second appreciation in an hour qualifies as "gushing," then that person has a serious problem. There are 360 ten-second chunks in every hour. All we want you to do, at first, is to take one of those 360 ten-second chunks of time, and use it to voice an appreciation.

Right now, look around yourself and let your eyes rest on something you can appreciate. Then, get out your notebook and fill in the blank below with an appreciation.

Right now I am appreciating _____ .
Keep the flow going with some even deeper appreciations.
One of the biggest appreciations I have about life on Earth is _____ .
I deeply appreciate myself for the way _____ .
(Thinking of someone you are intimate with) I deeply appreciate _____ *for the way they* _____ .

See how many things, qualities, and people you can appreciate. When you have completed your list, go out into the world and begin to become aware of other things you appreciate, and see if you can voice one appreciation an hour for the rest of the day. Then continue this process into the future for as long as it is pleasurable for you. What I think you will find is that the process of voicing appreciations will be one of the best possible means you have discovered to increase the amount of enjoyment you experience in your life. ♥

CHAPTER
TEN

Real-World Rule Number Three:
Listen Without Interrupting People, Including Yourself

LISTENING MIGHT BE the most important skill in nurturing an ongoing flow of love and good feelings in close relationships. When you interrupt someone, you are not giving them space to communicate their thoughts. If they cannot communicate their thoughts to you, not only will you be creating unnecessary conflict in your relationship, but you will also be missing one of the greatest rewards of being in a relationship—and that is coming to know your partner's similarities and their differences. And one of the best rewards of this process is that you will instantly receive valuable feedback from your partner that will benefit not only your relationship, but every aspect of your life.

Good listening is ultimately a whole-body skill, much like driving or swimming or skiing or riding a bike. Reading a manual helps you up to a point, but the real practice needs to take place behind the wheel or in the water or on the snow.

When most people think of effective listening, they usually think of it as a skill that has to do primarily with their ears, but when you tune in to your body sensitively, you can pick up subtle, but crucially important signals. Early in life, most of us learn to listen to the big, loud signals from our bodies—sensations such as hunger, pain, or the urges that propel us towards the bathroom. Later, if we put our minds to it, we can learn to listen to quieter signals such as the lump in the throat that tells us we are feeling sad.

In relationships, we need to learn to listen with our ears, while simultaneously being attuned to the subtler signals from the depths of ourselves and the people around us. For example, you might be listening to a friend talk about her difficulties with someone at work. Something she says triggers sympathy in you, which in turn triggers sadness and anxiety. If you are not attuned to your own body as you listen to her with your ears, you miss out on crucial parts of the conversation.

It is also helpful to remember to breathe while you are listening to people. Breathing helps you stay in the flow of the conversation. If you are in touch with your breathing, you can also give breathing space to others. People especially like it when you pause briefly after they finish speaking before you rush in with your point of view. Being in touch with your breathing also helps you stay open to your own feelings as you listen to others.

Another popular listening skill is to simply summarize what someone has just said. This can be a very informal summary, but one that tells them that you have been listening to them and that they have been heard. A skillful summary can also help clarify the central or most important issues for the speaker as well, who may be unable to see the larger picture because they are lost in a whirlwind of feelings and unprocessed details. This can be as simple as saying, "So, what I'm hearing you say is that you're feeling impatient with your coworkers" or "So, you would like Joe to at least call when he knows he's going to be late for dinner." Sometimes active listening is the best thing you can do for someone—when you encourage them to talk and you give them your full attention, they can often talk themselves out of a problem or into a solution without any other assistance from you.

Another very powerful benefit to active listening is illustrated in a story I call "The Party."

THE PARTY

A friend of ours went to a party where he would be meeting his wife's coworkers from her new job for the first time. He felt anxious as the time for the party grew near, and wondered whether they would like him or not. He also noticed that he was rehearsing various scenarios in his mind in which he tried in different ways to impress them. But on the way to the party, he decided that, instead of trying to impress anyone, he would spend the evening simply listening to them and summarizing what they had just said. Immediately he felt himself relax and the anxiety melt out of his body.

At the party, he spent the evening listening carefully to everyone, responding with phrases like "If I understand what you're saying, you feel strongly that ..." and "Let me see if I understand what you mean ..." He also avoided voicing his own opinions, even though at times it meant biting his tongue to keep from doing so.

To his amazement, he discovered that no one noticed or remarked on the fact that he was just listening. Each person he talked to during the evening seemed content to be listened to without interruption. On the way home, his wife (whom he had not told about the experiment) told him that a number of people had made a point of telling her what a remarkable person he was. The word "charismatic" was used by one person to describe him, while another said he was one of the most "articulate" people she had ever met.

Could it be that charisma and brilliance have as much to do with how we listen as what we say? Imagine a world in which people actually listen to each other, rather than just waiting for the other people to stop talking so they can give their opinion.

You can test this process right now. Close your eyes and take a few breaths and give a simple summary of what you have just learned in this chapter. ♥

CHAPTER
ELEVEN

Real-World Rule Number Four: Practice Impeccable Integrity

HERE IS HOW to keep your life simple and flowing with energy: do what you say you are going to do, and do not do what you say you are not going to do.

This is especially important in your close relationships, because one of the most common ways for someone to sabotage a relationship is by a breach of integrity. Often this occurs when the flow of positive energy is so new and unfamiliar to one of the partners that they experience fear and nervousness instead of appreciation. A broken agreement is a common way to sabotage this flow of positive energy and recreate a situation of tension and resentment that feels more familiar—and less threatening. The first broken agreement often begins a downward spiral of struggling and distrust that ends in the dissolution of what could have been a valuable relationship. And then the whole process of self-sabotage repeats in the next relationship.

In the ideal world, all of us would keep our agreements by doing what we say we are going to do and not doing what we have said we would not do, but in the real world, most of us will not get to impeccable integrity today or tomorrow, so we also need to know what to do when we fall short. Nobody is perfect. Until we get that way, let us work at creating a life in which we strive for impeccable integrity, but also know how to handle it as quickly as possible whenever we fall short.

If you find you are not going to be able to keep an agreement, have a conversation with the key person to find out if you can change the agreement. If you realize too late that you have already failed to keep an agreement, make amends for the broken promise in any way possible that seems fair to everyone involved.

As an exercise, think back over the last couple of days and see if you can remember an example of being impeccable about keeping an agreement. This would be an instance in which you did exactly what you promised someone you would do.

Now, see if you can remember a situation over the last couple of days in which you were less than impeccable; a situation where you failed to do something you said you were going to do, or you did something you said you would not do.

The goal of this exercise is not to beat yourself up for anything you did while not fully conscious or impeccable. The goal is to become impeccable, and the first step to impeccability is to see things exactly as they are. Once you realize this, you will know that all of the attention you put into this exercise will rapidly accelerate your path to not only full consciousness but also to impeccability itself.

Now, think back over your life. Are there people in your life to whom you have failed to keep agreements? Is there anyone to whom you feel you need to make amends? Get out your notebook and make a list, as follows:

One person I need to make amends with is _____.

Then, after you fill in the blank, make a plan for how you might make amends with that person:

I will _____ to make amends with them.

Sometimes this can be as simple as a phone call to acknowledge the remorse you feel for having failed to keep your agreements. Sometimes you may feel the need for more than just a phone call. Be sure to include a deadline for taking action to remedy the situation. To handle it immediately is often best, while you are still actively feeling remorse. If you wait too long, sometimes nothing happens, which would deny you the benefits of having made amends. ♥

CHAPTER
TWELVE

How to Make a Genuine Connection with Someone
You Are Attracted to in the First Ten Seconds

NOW THAT YOU have followed this step-by-step process of the inner work necessary to attracting genuine love into your life, and the four real world rules for success in life and love, you are ready to take the most important step in finding your future partner—but this step is one of the most misunderstood in the whole process—and this step is reaching out and connecting with that future partner in a way that guarantees success.

One of the most frustrating things in attracting genuine love into your life is that feeling of awkwardness that keeps you from being able to make a good connection when you first meet someone to whom you are attracted. But, once you learn a few simple Do's and Don't's, you can strike up a conversation with a stranger without fear. The resulting experience for both of you will be one of ease and pleasure, and you will actually begin to look forward to situations where you might meet new people.

The first thing to be aware of is that the first ten seconds of connecting with someone is the most important ten seconds of the entire relationship. In fact, these first ten seconds often determine whether there will be any relationship at all. In these first ten seconds, you will learn quite a bit about the other person as well—often enough to know whether they are someone you are interested in getting to know better, or if, in fact, they exhibit any of the qualities you have already determined you do not want to experience in your intimate relationships ever again.

We are going to focus in detail on the first ten seconds of meeting someone to whom you are attracted. In the following example, the two people meeting are a male and a female, although you could just as easily substitute a same-sex interaction. The dynamics are the same, no matter what genders or sexual orientations are involved.

You are shopping in a supermarket, pushing your cart along in the produce section. You are deciding which cantaloupe to buy, taking your time to sniff or heft or do whatever you do to make a good selection. Out of the corner of your eye, you notice a person looking over the nectarines in a nearby bin. You experience a feeling of attraction to that person, so you take a closer, longer look. She glances your way, makes eye contact, and smiles.

Now, everything in the preceding paragraph took place in four seconds or less. What you do over the next six seconds—especially what you say and how you say it—makes a profound difference.

Here is what the majority of people say in these all-important six seconds: nothing. The moment passes because they feel awkward about saying something to establish deeper contact. They walk away, feeling disappointed in themselves for not being able to make a good connection. A small percentage of people actually say something, but it comes out awkwardly, and the other person does not respond positively. A tiny percentage of people say something that establishes a positive contact with the other person.

Often when people meet, they are yearning for deep connection, but this yearning has often brought them pain, embarrassment, rejection, and suffering. As a result, they are afraid of being conned, lied to, or manipulated again. Their fear is a way to protect themselves against further pain.

If you begin with something false or artificial, that is often the way the relationship goes. However, if you begin on a footing of authenticity, you create a template for the future that is based on truth and clarity. Here is exactly what to say and do:

Say something simple that is unarguably true. Even better, say something simple that is unarguably true and that you are experiencing in the moment. Here is an example of a simple statement you could say that meets those two criteria: "I am having a hard time deciding which cantaloupe to buy."

This statement may sound ridiculously simple to you, but it instantly establishes trust, because it shares something personal and non-threatening about you, and it cannot be interpreted as any kind of lie, con, or attempted manipulation.

Likewise, contrast these two statements:

Statement One: "I am having a hard time deciding which cantaloupe to choose."

Statement Two: "Do you know a good way to tell which cantaloupes are good?"

Our research has shown time after time that Statement Two turns people off, while Statement One turns them on. Can you see why?

The reason is that Statement Two reveals nothing about the speaker, yet asks the other person to reveal information. (Even simple information, like the way to judge a cantaloupe, is asking the person to step forward to a degree of intimacy that the speaker has not volunteered.)

If you say "I am having a hard time deciding which cantaloupe to choose," you create an opening that the other person can enter if he or she chooses. At the same time, you reveal something of yourself, while speaking the absolute, unarguable truth. There is no way another person could argue with your statement. They also feel at ease, because you have not lied, conned, or manipulated them.

Let us look at another example. You are standing near the punch bowl at a party. An interesting-looking man comes up beside you. You glance at him and he smiles.

Him: Hi.
You: Hi.
Him: Great party, huh?
You: Yes. Diane and Jim are such a great couple!
Him: Is the punch good?
You: How could it not be?

This type of interaction is not likely to produce instant trust and likeability. It reveals nothing about either person, and there is no hint of the kind of unarguable authenticity that makes for good connection. Instead, this is a mask-to-mask communication, rather than a heart-to-heart one.

Now, look at the same situation, but replace the phony, mask-to-mask dialogue with authenticity.

Him: Hi.

You: Hi.

Him: I notice you're looking at the punch bowl.

You: Yes, I'm trying to decide whether I want any or not.

Him: Me, too. Sometimes it's got alcohol in it, and I'm not a drinker.

You: Hmmm, I hadn't thought about that. I was wondering if it was loaded with sugar.

Him: Let's go find out.

You: Great. By the way, my name's . . .

Speaking unarguable truths is the ideal way to begin a relationship. There are two good reasons why. First, as we mentioned, the first ten seconds is a template for how the rest of the relationship will go. The second reason is equally important: speaking the truth will often flush out people who do not have a capacity or an interest in honest relationships. It is better to learn that in the first ten seconds than to take ten years of pain and suffering to learn the same lesson. For instance, imagine saying to a person you just met, "I am trying to decide which cantaloupe to choose," and the other person says, "Here, I will do it for you." Beware! This person is a Controller. They make bad partners. Or imagine that another person responds by saying in a mocking tone, "Geez, everybody knows that! What's wrong with you?" Beware! This person is a Critic. They make bad partners, too. If, however, the person responds in an authentic way that comes from their heart in the present moment, you know that you have met someone who will make for a good partner.

The best instruction I know about what to do when you first meet someone you are attracted to is to stay in the present moment. Do not attempt to repeat anything you have ever done before, and do not say anything you have ever said before. Say only simple and unarguably true things, such as "I am feeling warm in here" and "I feel nervous being here." If you can establish the relationship on the firm ground of authenticity—even ten seconds of it—you have a foundation on which you can build a mansion.

It is always that simple and that easy. Do not take our word for it, though. Now it is time for you to go out and get busy meeting new people. You will likely be amazed at the results you get. ♥

CHAPTER
THIRTEEN

Reprogramming Your Bio-computer

THE HUMAN BRAIN is the most marvelous creation we know of, and most of us are using only a tiny percentage of its power. Imagine that someone gave you a Lear jet when you were born, but as you grew up, the people around you told you it was only good for plowing potato fields. A Lear jet can fly at incredible speeds, but because of your early programming, you merely taxi it up and down the same bumpy rows every year, harvesting spuds.

One of the greatest things about human beings is our ability to reprogram ourselves. In this way, we can lift ourselves out of any kind of life we have had up until now, and launch ourselves into a new life by claiming certain concepts and ideas as our own. For example, even if you have been wounded in a close relationship in the past, and have shut down, you can decide to open to the flow of love again, and gradually rise out of your old programming into what you really want now.

The process of Whole-Body Learning that we have used throughout this program is one way to reprogram your bio-computer. Programming new and better ideas into your consciousness will counteract the effects of the limited ideas we were programmed with when we were growing up. To speed up this process, I have included a specially-designed guided session as Track Seven on the enclosed CD. You can use this every day to increase the speed and depth of this reprogramming to bring genuine love into your life. On Track Seven, I give you six concepts that we have found useful to float through your mind every day. We also recommend that you write these concepts down and post them in different places that you frequent during your daily routine, such as on your dashboard or your refrigerator or beside your bed. The six concepts we will be using are:

LISTEN TO TRACK 7
Reprogramming Your
Bio-computer

1. *I give and receive love effortlessly.*
2. *Genuine love comes to me effortlessly.*
3. *I feel loved and loving all the time.*
4. *I release the pain of my unpleasant experiences in love.*
5. *I commit to loving and feeling loved all the time.*
6. *I live in expanding waves of love and creativity.*

PROJECTING YOURSELF INTO THE FUTURE

As we move toward the end of our journey together, I want to leave you with one final very powerful activity that will help make the process of attracting genuine love into your life happen in a smooth, rapid manner. Before I do that, I want to give you my sincere thanks for your willingness to open up this territory in yourself.

The importance of the love that we have been talking about in this program is actually the foundation for a much larger task we have in this life. At some point in our lives, we begin to be called on to love and accept all of the parts of ourselves that we have not embraced in the past. In this way, every moment of life becomes an opportunity to learn more deeply how to love ourselves.

But it does not stop there. As we learn to love ourselves more deeply, we begin to attract new types of people into our lives—people who can help us learn how to interact with others from a foundation of love. As this becomes a larger and larger part of our lives, our great challenge becomes how to learn to be more open in those moments—not only be open to the love inside ourselves reaching out, but also to remain open to the love that others bring to us.

It is in this sense that the greatest challenge in our lives is the one we have been exploring together—that is, the willingness to open up and attract into our lives the kind of love that we most desire. When that happens, the true and much broader path of love opens for us as well.

Finding genuine love has changed my life more profoundly than I ever imagined possible, and I wish you the greatest of success, not only in finding genuine love, but in learning how to apply this process in every area of your life.

And now, as your final exercise in this program, I invite you to listen to Track Eight, "Projecting into Your Future." This very powerful process helps you take the energy of your present experience and project it into an imaginary future, so that when you start to receive more love in your life, you can open up and enjoy it, rather than reverting to old patterns of pushing it away or not allowing it in. ♥

LISTEN TO TRACK 8
Projecting into the Future

We hope you have learned a great deal about yourself in the course of this program. Changing your programming about love is bound to stir up new levels of agony and ecstasy in your life. You will probably experience moments of great despair and moments of great hope. You may feel full of confusion and full of elation, all at once. All of these feelings (and whatever else you experience) are healthy signs of real growth. You can be proud of yourself for your courage in taking on the task of attracting genuine love.

We invite you to go through the material again as often as you like. Doing the lessons again can deepen the experience and the benefits.

If, by now, you have brought into your life the relationship you were seeking, congratulations! Please drop us a line and tell us the story of how it happened. One of the great pleasures of our lives is reading letters and emails from people who have attracted a beautiful new relationship into their lives as a result of applying the material in this program.

In closing, we would like to express our deep appreciation to you for joining us on the incredible adventure of attracting genuine love. May you be richly blessed on this journey of a lifetime.

With love and respect,
Gay Hendricks
Kathlyn Hendricks

The Hendricks Institute
402 W. Ojai Avenue, Suite 101-413
Ojai, CA 93023
agl@hendricks.com

A Gift to My Ideal Partner: Some Helpful Things to Know About Me

If you bring a new toaster or computer home with you, you will likely find an owner's manual or set of operating instructions packed in with your new acquisition. It gives you helpful hints on how to get the most out of it, as well as information about how to avoid disasters that require repair. Our toaster oven came with a thirty-two-page booklet full of helpful hints such as (believe it or not) "Do not immerse your toaster oven in water for any reason."

It would be nice if we all came with such a guide. If we did, the people who come into our lives would not have to learn all of our rules, preferences, and hot buttons the hard way. In our own relationship, Kathlyn and I decided to make an owner's manual for each other, to save the wear and tear of trial-and-error learning. It also turned out to be helpful in getting to know ourselves better, as well as introducing the other person to our likes, dislikes, and quirks.

INSTRUCTIONS

Do not write in this book. We suggest you go out and buy a new notebook or journal and handwrite the following information as a gift to your partner. If you are not yet in a new relationship, imagine giving this information to the ideal partner you would like to attract into your life. If you are already in a close relationship, consider actually giving it as a gift to the one you are with presently. Add anything else to this list that you would like your lover to know about you. Be honest, be thorough, and have fun.

MY DAY

I like to get up around _____.

If you were listening to the sounds of my house in the morning, you would probably hear _____ (e.g., silence, children, radio, TV, music, etc.).

My favorite toothpaste is _____ and I squeeze the tube _____ (from the bottom, from the top, or randomly).

For breakfast I like to have _____.

My favorite lunch is _____ .

My ideal dinner is _____.

My favorite meal of the day is _____.

My favorite foods are _____.

My favorite snacks are _____.

My favorite desserts are _____.

My favorite drinks are _____.

I absolutely cannot stand the following foods _____.

If I could only take one thing to a desert island to eat for a year, it would
probably be _____.

I _____ (like/do not like) to cook.

(If you like to cook) My favorite foods to cook are _____.

In the evenings, I like to _____.

My favorite televisions shows are _____.

I usually go to bed around _____.

The side of the bed I prefer is _____.

I thrive on _____ hours of sleep a night.

FAVORITE PEOPLE AND THINGS

A few of my all-time favorite movies are _____.

The best books I have ever read are _____.

My favorite season of the year is _____.

My best friend is _____.

Some of my favorite people to be around are _____.

If I could pick a circle of friends from historical people, some of them
would be _____.

My favorite recreation activities are _____.

The best place I have ever been on vacation is _____.

Of the places I have not been to yet, I think I would most like to
visit _____.

UN-FAVORITE PEOPLE AND THINGS

The kind of movies I am most likely to avoid are _____.

You probably will not ever see me reading _____.

I go out of my way to avoid being around the kind of people who _____.

Some of my pet peeves are _____.

INTIMACY

From my early family life I learned about relationships that _____.

Of the relationships I have personally been around, the one or ones I would choose as
    role models are _____.

In my own intimate relationships, the biggest complaints I have had
    are _____.

The biggest complaints they have had about me are _____.

A "deal-breaker" for me in a relationship is _____.

Another thing I do not think I could tolerate in a relationship is _____.

What I most treasure in a close relationship is _____.

DREAMS, SPIRIT, VISIONS

My spiritual life is _____.

As a child I dreamed of _____

My biggest as-yet-unfulfilled dream is to _____.

My vision for what I will be doing five years from now is _____.

About the Authors

GAY HENDRICKS RECEIVED his Ph.D. in psychology from Stanford in 1974, and taught in the School of Education at the University of Colorado, retiring after 20 years of service. He is the founder of two organizations, The Hendricks Institute and the Foundation for 21st-Century Leadership. Dr. Hendricks is the author of more than 20 books, including the national bestsellers Conscious Living and The Corporate Mystic.

Kathlyn Hendricks has been a pioneer in the field of body-mind integration for over thirty years. She received her doctorate in psychology in 1982, and has been a member of the Academy of Dance/Movement Therapists of the American Dance Therapy Association since 1975. She is the co-author of ten books, including Conscious Loving and The Conscious Heart, and the author of a book of poetry, A Waterbaby Contemplates Dry Land.

CD SESSIONS

1. The Commitment Meditation 6:40

2. Uncovering Your Unconscious Commitments 7:13

3. The Body Scan 15:15

4. Breathing into Fear 11:23

5. Learning to Love Yourself Meditation 12:29

6. Going Public with Your Commitment 9:31

7. Reprogramming Your Bio-computer 7:36

8. Projecting into the Future 7:56